Balancing Your Orbit

Balancing Your Orbit

Harnessing the Heavens

How to Use Planetary Energies to Manifest Your Dreams

Kathy Kerston
International Astrologer & Metaphysician
Director of The Institute for Spiritual Development

iUniverse, Inc.
New York   Bloomington

Balancing Your Orbit
Harnessing the Heavens
How to Use Planetary Energies to Manifest Your Dreams

Copyright © 2008 by Kathy Kerston

All rights reserved. No part of this book may be used or reproduced by any means, graphic, electronic, or mechanical, including photocopying, recording, taping or by any information storage retrieval system without the written permission of the publisher except in the case of brief quotations embodied in critical articles and reviews.

iUniverse books may be ordered through booksellers or by contacting:

iUniverse
1663 Liberty Drive
Bloomington, IN 47403
www.iuniverse.com
1-800-Authors (1-800-288-4677)

Because of the dynamic nature of the Internet, any Web addresses or links contained in this book may have changed since publication and may no longer be valid.

The views expressed in this work are solely those of the author and do not necessarily reflect the views of the publisher, and the publisher hereby disclaims any responsibility for them.

ISBN: 978-0-595-47717-3 (pbk)
ISBN: 978-0-595-91979-6 (ebk)

Printed in the United States of America

Gentle Disclaimer

This book was written by a right-brained person, for right-brained people. My apologies to left-brained people, who might find a little difficulty trusting their right brain to take them on a fascinating journey into the realm where miracles happen … the realm of the right brain. I promise you, my left-brain friends, should you choose to explore, you will find resources inside yourself you never knew existed. Don't analyze and question; just accept, journey, and enjoy.

Most of the stories and myths that I use in this book are my interpretation from the many books that I have read on Greek Mythology, and mainly from my memory as well as other varied sources. I have used these stories in my work as an astrologer for over thirty-five years to help my clients understand what the symbols in their astrology charts mean. If your interest lies in mythology, there are many good books on the market that you can refer to. The intention of this book is simply to use the planetary energies in a playful way to empower your life. Become as a child; explore your imagination, and use the power that lies within you to manifest your dreams.

This book is dedicated to all my clients,
whose constant questions forced
me to stretch my paradigms.

To my husband, Pat, whose journey
on this earthly plane demonstrated the
concepts in this book.

To my sons, Frank and Dan,
my daughters-in-law, Renee and Karen,
and my grandchildren,
Gianna, Frankie, Olivia, Ally, and Sofia,
whose love and support is always
a source of great joy.

To Anna Marie, who patiently proofed for me.

To Jill, without whom this book would still
be in my head.

Contents

xi	Preface
xiii	Introduction
1	MEET MERCURY
8	MEET VENUS
15	MEET MARS
19	MEET JUPITER
24	MEET SATURN
28	MEET URANUS
33	MEET NEPTUNE
37	MEET PLUTO
42	Additional Thoughts

Preface

Throughout my many, many years as an astrologer, I've encouraged my clients to focus on the great possibilities in their charts. Oftentimes people will say, "Kathy only tells you the good stuff." It is true, for the most part I do. Why, you ask. I realized very early on, and partly through looking at my own chart, sometimes with horror, that I could tell a client of wonderful opportunities, but if I gave them one little period where caution might be needed, that was the thing they focused on: "Saturn is out to get me."

I look at the birth chart as a script we wrote before we incarnated ourselves on this planet, a script that describes what we chose to experience. I believe that we have moved into an evolutionary state of awareness, and as such, we should look at this script and realize that we don't have to keep doing things the hard way. We wrote this script, and we can change it. We handed a copy of this script out to everyone who agreed to play a part in it, although, at the time, we might have been drinking too much wine with Neptune! I sometimes look in the mirror and say, "Kathy, you must have been out of your mind to write this chapter in your script." Then I laugh and say, "If I wrote it, I can change it, even if by just changing my perception, an act which will in itself yield incredible results."

When you accept that you wrote the script for your life, blame goes out the window. Don't waste time wondering why; that's not important, and it keeps you stuck in the past. As you forgive and move on, you absolve the others in your script and give them the choice to make changes in their own. As long as you hang on to "he did it," "she did it," "they did it," you are keeping this movie going in the same direction. And just a slight turn in the road can move you toward your dreams.

The power to change our lives is truly in our hands. Our creator gave us that power through our free will and our freedom of choice. Every day that we don't use our ability to create the life that we desire, we are shortchanging ourselves and those around us. It is our duty to ourselves not to allow the old belief systems to just pull us along on a path that we no longer wish to tread. The first step in any endeavor is always the most difficult and, of course, the most important.

Through an exercise of will, we can assume the position of director of our lives, but only when we choose to assume the responsibility.

Introduction

This revised edition came into being as a result of an experience I had when I was in the dream state. As an astrologer, hypnotherapist, and metaphysician for over thirty-five years, I have used my imagination to come up with creative ways for my clients to understand the effect the energies of the planets have on their lives. After seeing the results, and after receiving much prompting from my clients, I decided to write the book. About a year after I had written this book and gifted it to many of my clients, I had a powerful experience.

While in Europe and using these principles for a very important matter, I found myself, right before waking one morning, above the earth looking down at it, the view that an astronaut would see. I became aware of a presence that told me that I had done well in writing the book, but that in order to get the most out of the information, one would have to do the work from up here. When I inquired as to where I was, I was asked to think and answer my own question, to which I replied that I believed I was standing out of time. "Very good," was the response from the presence. "But how did I get here?" I again inquired. "How did you?" the presence replied. After considering for a moment, I responded, "Imagination." "Good," was the reply. "Imagination doesn't exist in linear time."

After affirming that I was correct, the presence went on to show me a very rudimental picture of the brain upon which it drew little circles that represented the program we had written before this incarnation, which one can read in the astrology chart. I was then shown all the planets beaming their energy toward the earth and our little programmed neurons picking up the vibration that we had chosen to experience. I was told that by going into the realm of imagination, and therefore out of linear time, we could change that program and thus choose to draw to ourselves the positive energy of any given planet. The planet doesn't decide it's out to get you; it is we who attract any given energy.

After awakening, and before attending the important undertaking that was in front of me, I used these principles in the following situation and achieved incredible results.

I was scheduled to appear in court to answer depositions in a lawsuit that I was pursuing. As I took my shower that morning, I imagined that I was calling on Saturn to give me wisdom, Mercury to help me articulate clearly, and Jupiter to give me the faith and optimism to know that the judge would rule justly.

It occurred to me after the third question that the judge had asked the same question in different ways. I took a deep breath, looked directly at the judge, and said in a very calm but effective manner, "Maybe, your Honor, I can answer your questions this way." I then proceeded to enlighten him on what he really should be asking. His eyes were wide open, as were my attorney's eyes. The judge took a large drink of water and didn't go anywhere near those questions again, and in the end, I won the case. When I asked my attorney later why he was looking as surprised as the judge, he told me that during depositions, you can only answer yes or no, not give a discourse like I did. However, my delivery was so intense, it seemed, that the judge was taken aback and didn't have the presence to stop me, and as a result, I was able to state my case very clearly. By trusting that I could harness the gifts that the planets personify, I was able to project clearly to the judge what my position was, thus assuring myself a just ruling.

If you are reading this book, you have most likely begun your journey to self-awakening, and as part of this awakening, you most likely have accepted that you are a cocreator with the divine. To keep things simple, I will refer to the creator, the universal divine, as God. Many of us who were raised in the Judeo-Christian tradition were taught to believe that God created the universe: the Sun, the Moon, and the planets. We were also taught that we were created in God's image, that we are all children of God. If we came into being by the same hand that formed the universe, why is it that we cringe when we look up our horoscope in the newspaper or are told by an astrologer that the planets are at stressful angles in the heavens and are affecting our lives?

I'll tell you why. We've given away our divinity; instead we stand mutely accepting whatever life decides to dish out. "It's our fate," we bemoan. "It's all in the stars." Sorry, that's just another cop out. Certainly it's true that some things are preordained, but we must always remember that we have the incredible gift of free will. Acknowledging the fact that we have free will gives us an advantage, along with the ability to test our ingenuity to find out if we really are divine beings.

All right, so we have free will. In fact we've always had it. Don't you think it's about time we wake up and use this wonderful gift? For too long we've behaved like a group of pathetic creatures, blaming our fate on our parents, teachers, friends, circumstances, and, yes, even the stars.

Well, this is now going to stop! The solution is right in your hand. You're holding a powerful tool that will help you to take charge and make changes in your life! You're going to take control and get results.

Just as we have distinct personalities with strengths and weaknesses, so do the planets, and you're going to learn how to make them work to effect change in your life. We've always had this resource just within our grasp, but up until now, we had no idea how to put it to use.

First, we must find out who and what we're going to be dealing with. This guide will introduce you to these different planetary energies, and then you can decide how best to make them work for you!

Many of the roots of astrology are lost in antiquity, but the association within the planetary energies has been wonderfully displayed for us through mythology. Mythology is a good way to look at the characteristics and energies of the planets through their association with, and embodiment of, the gods and goddesses. Different cultures have their own way of depicting mythology to explain a series of beliefs about cosmic mysteries and the beings who represent those beliefs. For most of us, Greek and Roman mythology is best known. While astrology has assigned the Roman names to the planets, the myths referred to are almost always from Greek Mythology. The Greeks gave the gods, which the planets are named after, human qualities such that they were both *benefic* (beneficial) and *malefic* (detrimental). The Greeks also made it clear that the gods were in charge, and only if we pleaded with them would they offer us any assistance. Today we know better. All of the planets have power. The idea is to learn what powers they possess and how those traits can be used to benefit you.

A question that I have been asked on more than one occasion is, "Am I giving more power to these planets than to God?" Your answer is "yes" if you allow them, or anything else, to run your life. You are created in God's image; therefore, you should behave as a true child of God would. Do this by using that power with which you are endowed—free will—to create good in your life and in the lives of others. By taking control of your life, you're honoring not just yourself, but also your maker.

Look at our world. We've certainly used enough energy creating a lot of misery, and then we have the nerve to blame God! We declare that all the negative results were "his will." Thank god (no pun intended) that the mind of our creator is so far above our petty interpretations of what he, she, or it would or would not think about something, that he's probably amused.

"Why a book about talking to the planets?" you may ask.

"This is nonsense," you might say.

"Do you really think for a moment that I believe these deities, as you call them, are up there listening to me? Even if they are, how can I be sure they're not going to get bent out of shape and do something nasty if I start demanding that they do what I say?"

"Do what I say?" my client Joe asked when I introduced him to the concept of using planetary energies and explained that I was writing this book. Clearly, he was being influenced by Saturn's paranoia of losing his supreme power. When I told him to command Saturn to shove his paranoia elsewhere, he looked at me with alarm.

"Oh, Kathy, what if he really gets mad?" he asked. I couldn't help laughing and went on to explain to him how I personify these planets. I have done this by thinking of them as the gods and goddesses in Greek mythology. I much prefer to imagine that I am addressing a beautiful goddess than a faceless energy source when I want the help of Venus. And I simply love dancing with Mars to rid myself of pent-up anger.

In this book we'll meet each planet and get an idea of how to employ their energies. Take Uranus as an example. Among all of the planets, Uranus is like an electric source of power in the universe. Now, we all know that electricity comes into our homes on a wire that connects into an electric outlet. Once it's in the house, it's our choice what we use it for. We can plug into a television, DVD player, VCR, or stereo for entertainment. We can plug a night-light, an answering machine, or a sewing machine into an outlet. Or you can choose that appliance that you know is a hazard because it has a frayed wire and could cause a short or maybe even a fire. The energy is there, but how we apply it is our choice. This guide to the characteristics of each planet's energy will teach you how to visualize energies and harness their unique powers to empower yourself to achieve your goals.

The first principle to understand is that there are metaphysical laws in the world, just as there are physical laws. While we may not be able to stop the storm, we can put up a lightening rod. Let's say, for example, that we know by observing our astrological chart that the planetary energies are such that they herald a time when our resources will be tight and it would be prudent for us to economize. At this time, we would state out loud that we will take care of our resources now with an absolute conviction that abundance will flow to us in a positive manner, that whatever we have chosen to learn has been learned, and we are now ready for abundance in our lives. In doing this, we're not stopping the energies of caution, but directing them in a positive way.

Balancing Your Orbit

Let us now discover the energies of these planets and talk about how you can harness their power. It's time to let go of limiting thoughts and attitudes and take back control of your life. Throw Saturn's paranoia out the door, along with that idiot that you have been trying to save with your codependency traits (residue from the age of Pisces), and have fun! It's very rewarding to improve yourself and then witness the positive effect it has on every aspect of your life. Remember, when you become the best that you can be, everyone gains! Now it's time to meet the planets. Good luck and enjoy!

MEET MERCURY
THE GREAT COMMUNICATOR

Mercury is the Roman equivalent of the Greek god Hermes. This Peter Pan of the zodiac is a wonderful guy with many talents. When Mercury was born, according to the Homeric Hymns, a group of ancient hymns in Greek mythology, the first thing he did was steal his brother's cows. Mercury denied the act and was summoned to Olympus to be judged. Because he was so disarming and cute, he charmed his father and brothers and was forgiven for his childish prank, but it became known that he could use his wits for good or bad. Referred to as the messenger, it was his job to travel between Olympus (heaven or higher self), Earth (the physical world), and Hades (the underworld and death).

Mercury is always depicted as forever young, a winged, youthful god who has the ability to time-travel in the blink of an eye and change course on a dime. For Mercury, language is no barrier; his mental abilities are such that he can see both sides of a situation almost at the same time, which confuses those who can only see one point of view. Because he remains always a youth, his mind is constantly curious, his manner alert and often juvenile and jovial, as he seeks new information and the chance to communicate it to others.

Mercury sees his mental versatility as his trademark, and he refuses to be placed in a restricting mold. Because he is so versatile, the other gods are amused and tolerate many of his childish pranks. Aware of Mercury's penchant for mischief, the old alchemists always prayed that their minds would be guided for the higher good when employing the brilliance of Mercury in their work. While our job is to honor the great gifts that

Balancing Your Orbit

Mercury bestows upon us, we have to be diligent and aware that he can be alternately serious, prankish, and even downright dishonest. Though some might call him a trickster, a con artist, and even a liar, no one would deny that he also has a serious side. He has an incredibly quick mind and the ability to communicate his thoughts with ease; he is the alchemist, the healer, and the literary genius. In the body, he rules the nervous system, the lungs, and the breath we need to survive.

Mercury holds the privileged ability of being able to travel into the underworld, where he escorts souls after death. The soul journeys into the underworld to be transformed and renewed. Few are allowed to return from this dark domain in their present form, but Mercury can. Why? Because Mercury understands that the way we choose to use our minds (our thoughts) dictates whether we will live in a paradise or a prison.

Mercury decides how we think and what we believe. Because of the fluidity of this planetary energy, there is no reason why we should have to remain stuck with old beliefs that do not serve us anymore. Mercury is acutely aware that to change our minds is to change our beliefs, thereby changing our lives; think a thought continually, and it becomes our reality.

An astrology chart, which maps the positions of the planets on the date and at the time and place of the birth of an individual, is divided into twelve sections, Aries is placed on the horizon, or first sector. The natural progression through the signs—Aries, Taurus, Gemini, and so forth—places Gemini, the sign ruled by Mercury, on the part of the chart that involves siblings, early environment, schooling, writing ability, modes of transportation, and early thinking patterns. It also shows one's aptitude to communicate effectively. The other part of the chart that Mercury rules involves work and health. Here we see Mercury as the apprentice. There are stories of him learning how to create musical instruments, including one where he fashioned a lyre from a tortoise shell, which he gave to his brother Apollo, thus bringing music to the world.

There are many pictures of Mercury with a caduceus, the symbol of the magical healer. Modern science has proven a strong connection between how we think and the state of our health. Any improvement in this area can have far-reaching effects, making a conversation with Mercury a must.

How do you have conversations with these planets? You can meditate, use your imagination to create a scene that is empowering and positive. You can treat these planets like imaginary friends that you talk to while doing the dishes, driving to work, showering. It is important that you come up with the way that works best for you.

Some of my clients have asked why I seem to order the planets around. "Why don't you ask nicely?" they inquired. The answer lies in the intention. I've realized that when I am moving energy, I get quicker results if I yell at the planet, thus stating my intention with force. When we speak clearly and with determination, we are making a positive statement to ourselves that what we want we have the ability to attract. Remember, when you pleaded with your mother, you knew you might not get what you wanted. For those who ask me where this attitude fits within their religious training, I quote them various forms of the statement "Ask and it shall be given." As far as I can remember, it wasn't stated, "Maybe, if you're good or if I feel like giving it to you." I leave you to answer this for yourself.

When should you have a talk with Mercury? Here are some situations where his influence might be called for:

- When you need to write an effective letter. Imagine the paper or computer in front of you. See Mercury touching your brow with his hand. Imagine that he is writing the letter, and then say, "Right now, Mercury, you're going to sharpen my writing skills so that I may communicate my thoughts in a clear and concise manner."
- When you seek answers to questions. Imagine that you have written the question down and are handing it to the winged god, and say, "Mercury, bring the thoughts that lead me to the correct answer to

this question. My mind is bright and alert, and I eagerly await your response."
- When you want to articulate your thoughts well in an important situation. Imagining that you are already there, see the winged god by your shoulder, and tell him, "We have an important situation to handle here. Heighten my ability to think clearly, accurately, and intelligently. Give me your superb gift of fluidity of speech so that I may articulate effectively."
- When you need to think on your feet. "Hey, Mercury, give me your quick-as-lightening thoughts. Illuminate my mind with brilliance so that I may always think on my feet."
- When you are getting ready to travel. Imagine Mercury making your travel plans in such a way that you know that everything has been handled well. See yourself happy and contented with the plans and how they are being made. "OK, Mercury, we are taking a trip and it is going to be a great one. I know you have orchestrated everything and all will go smoothly."
- Whenever you need quickness of mind and agile action. Call on Mercury and say, "Let's move it, Mercury. Give me swift, fluid action. Let my thoughts and ideas come quickly and accurately."
- When you need to think positively about your health. Say to Mercury, "Oh, great healer, I am choosing to be healthy and happy. Keep me focused on positive thoughts. Help me choose uplifting ideas, attitudes, and situations. Bring me positive information that will keep me healthy."
- When you need to make changes in your work environment. Sit quietly and imagine yourself in a work situation that truly makes you happy. Tell Mercury that this is what you want. As you imagine what you want, putting as many details in the scene as you can, say, "Mercury, when my mind wanders from this scene, remind me that what I think creates my realty. Keep me focused."

- When you want to let go of old thought patterns. Tell Mercury to erase those old memories that are circulating just beneath the surface of your consciousness. Tell him the thoughts are adding nothing positive to the present and you want them removed.
- When you want excitement and versatility in any situation. Tell Mercury it's time for fun. "Come on, Mercury, create some new and exciting ideas and situations." Invite Venus and Mars to come along, and then imagine, imagine, imagine. Have fun just thinking about it.
- When you want to improve relationships with siblings. Imagine a scene in which you create harmony with your siblings. Tell Mercury that this is how you choose to think of your siblings, that this is your new reality

Whenever important papers need to be signed, it is imperative that you call on Mercury and ask him to bring in the additional energies of Jupiter and Saturn. You'll want Jupiter's assistance because he rules legal matters and always brings an optimistic outcome. Saturn is necessary because he brings caution, dignity, and seriousness to any situation. So, here are the words to use when you talk to Mercury. These are only a few samples, feel free to make up your own.

If you find that you're caught up in saying unflattering things about others, just say to Mercury, "Mercury, my friend, stop being so nasty! No more gossiping and exaggerating the truth. Stop making life more complicated and difficult. I want you to help me, not hinder me!"

- "You will help me write that play I have been dreaming about." "I'm ready to give that important speech." "I'm ready to embark on a career in communications."

- "You're now going to quicken my ability to comprehend all that I hear, read, and observe. The assistance that you give me will be stored in my brain to be accessed with ease when I need it!"
- "It's now time to stop my mind from going off in all directions, scattering my thoughts and holding me back from doing what must be done. Help my thoughts to be original, organized, and productive."
- "When I choose to meditate, you will guide me into that deep unconscious realm where I will find wisdom and the answers to any questions I may have."

Definitely take Mercury and his colleagues to that important board meeting. Summon him when you know that it's time to open your mouth and speak up, and you want to get your words out without inserting your foot.

Whenever you feel your mind going in a million directions, Mercury's up to his tricks. This is when you have to tell him, in no uncertain terms, who is in charge and how he is going to apply some helpful energy, but by all means, don't forget to thank him! (All servants respond well to praise.) Here's a phrase that you may like to try, and do lay it on, as Mercury loves flattery: "Thank you, Mercury, forever young and smart, you incredible, lovable guy. I know you'll listen to my plea and serve me well!"

Well, now that you have an idea of how to handle the fleet-footed Mercury, let's get on with the next planet!

MEET VENUS
THE GODDESS OF LOVE

Venus was known as Aphrodite by the Greeks. She was considered the loveliest of all the goddesses on Olympus, the place the Greek gods call home. When we think of Venus, we may think of beauty, creativity, and the need to cocreate sexually or artistically. Most of all, however, when we think of Venus, we think of love and passion.

There are two versions of her birth. Homer, in *The Iliad*, places Aphrodite as the daughter of Zeus and a sea nymph, Dione, while Hesiod describes her as coming forth from the sea, fully grown, floating on a seashell, the result of the violent act that Cronus (Saturn) performed on his father (Uranus), when he cut off his genitals with a sickle. According to Hesiod, the genitals were tossed into the ocean, and as the sperm mixed with the ocean, it gave birth to Aphrodite.

It is interesting to note that both versions tie this goddess to the sea, Neptune's domain, and when Venus is found in an astrology chart to be occupying the sign of Pisces, which Neptune rules, she is considered to be in her most exalted state. As with all the planets, Venus has both a positive and a negative side, and it is in understanding her energies that you will be able to call forth her undeniable power. In a book that I highly recommend, *Goddesses in Everywoman,* by Jean Shinoda Bolen, Venus is referred to as the alchemic goddess, a description that fits this planet perfectly, as without her touch of magic, most creations seem sterile.

Without love and passion, we can become lethargic, but when our heart races and the adrenaline pumps with anticipation and enthusiasm, Venus comes to life. Venus rules two sections of a chart: the first represents self-earned money, valuables, and the value of one's self; the other area rules marriage and partnerships.

There are many stories of Venus's liaisons, but one very interesting story is of her affair with Mars (the Greek Ares). These two have an on-again, off-again relationship fired by passion. It is said that she birthed three children to Mars: Harmonia, Deimos, and Phobos (Harmony, Terror, and Fear). When the energies of Venus and Mars operate correctly, you have harmony, love, peace, and abundance. The other two, Fear and Terror, rear their heads when Venus is vain, jealous, or vindictive. In her relationship with Neptune, she nearly always behaves in a positive manner, yet even here, we have to watch that in her compassion she doesn't become too self-sacrificing.

Because of her love for the luxuries of life, her artistic expression, and her refined tastes, she is given rulership over money.

It's interesting to note that sometimes when money is a problem, it can be associated with a lack of self-value. Creativity is of equal importance, something which can be seen by her choice of husband. Aphrodite is married to Hera's lame son, Hephaestus, who can't understand why a goddess like her would love him, which is why he places his emotions into the beautiful objects he creates.

I often think of this story when I see a couple and hear people say, "What on earth does she (or he) see in that person?" What they see in the Hephaestus-person is someone with great creative energy, but when the Hephaestus-person can't accept the love that Venus offers, he/she will drive the Venus-person into other liaisons.

Because Venus has such enormous emotional power, she, more than any other planet, has the ability to create incredible magic. We all know that love and passion make the heart race, and she has the power to quicken the pulse, to invoke in us the desire to reach out to others. Now is the time to put that magical power to work. Don't let vanity or jealousy creep in and mess up your plans. Harness the Venus energy and create magic in your life.

The passion and love of Venus is not only for our personal relationships, for this beautiful goddess also has an affinity with many tools of the arts, and she can help you use them with more ease and confidence. Her voice is said to be sweet, due to her rulership of the sign Taurus, which rules the throat, and her presence is strong in the charts of singers. Her persuasive manner is what makes some feel the need to write a screenplay, sing an aria, paint a picture, or express any of the many faces of creativity.

With her love of the finer things in life, it's only fitting that she has rulership over money, since many of the things she likes come with a large price tag! She loves luxuriant and beautiful things and makes no bones about her preferences.

Call in abundance with a positive attitude; don't let Venus act like a self-indulgent, spoiled brat (who can, consequently, be quite immoral and very jealous). You take command.

So when should you call upon Venus? These are some of the times when it might be appropriate to give her a call:

- When you want to attract love, together with peace and harmony, into your life. Imagine that you are in a beautiful place having a conversation with this lovely goddess. Say something like, " Beautiful goddess, I embody all your positive attributes. Make me aware that I can give and attract love, peace, and harmony into my life. Let your light shine through my eyes and your harmony resonate in my voice."
- When Venus has just met Mars and the passions are flying. Imagine yourself approaching this encounter as a goddess. (If you are a man, you will be approaching Venus as Mars; be creative and change the scene.) "Beautiful goddess, we enter into this liaison with the intention (state whether you want it permanent or not) to give and receive love on all levels, physical, emotional, and spiritual. I am pure love, and I reflect this in all of my relationships."

Balancing Your Orbit

- When you would like to attract money. Imagine that you are sitting with your checkbook, or looking at your account online, and Venus is standing by your side. Know that her power is affecting the attraction of more resources. If you have a business, see new orders or checks being delivered. Imagine Venus empowering you to know that you are attracting more money.
- When you find yourself feeling jealous or resentful. Imagine Venus and say something like, "Come on, you incredible goddess, there is plenty of everything in the universe for everyone." Look at all the good things in your life, and you will attract more. Imagine Venus saying to you, "I love you, please love yourself."
- When you are acting like a spoiled brat. "Venus," you say, "this is not very ladylike, beautiful goddess." Laugh with her and tell her in no uncertain terms that you are elegant, and that she had better behave as such.
- When you need her to balance a situation where there is discord. Visualize yourself as surrounded by pink light. Feel as though the harmony of the universe is being directed to you. See yourself as emanating peace.
- When you're ready to decorate your home. Imagine Venus looking at the paint colors, picking out the style. Talk to her and ask her to guide your choices.
- When you have to perform on stage, especially if your talent is singing. Imagine yourself getting ready for a performance. Imagine that Venus is standing in front of you. As you prepare to go on stage, visualize her merging into your body, making all her talents yours. See yourself on stage, more magnificent than you have ever been, with your talent flowing from deep within, resulting in an incredible performance.
- When you have to paint that portrait or mold that dish or vase. Sit quietly with your arms outstretched and imagine Venus placing her arms and hands over yours. Then see the goddess touching your

heart, activating your creativity from deep within, and know that your work is inspired.
- When you're eating too much food or sweets (especially chocolate). When this happens, it's time to have a talk with the beautiful goddess. "Venus, I love my body, and I know that you love it too. Motivate me toward those healthy habits that will keep this body beautiful; return it to the state I desire." See yourself the way you want to be, and imagine that Venus is with you when you make choices. Listen to her.
- When you need to shop for something to wear to that special occasion or update your wardrobe. If you realize that your wardrobe is drab, lacking style or color, then it's definitely time to call on Venus. Take her shopping and talk to her as you make your choices. "Venus, this is a special occasion and I want to look magnificent. Help me find the right outfit."

If you have every color under the rainbow in your closet and your friends think you should return Joseph's coat of many colors to the Bible, you need to talk to Venus. Also, if your closets are bursting with clothes that you just keep buying but could not possibly wear in one lifetime, you need to talk to Venus. These situations are a clear indication that she's out of control. Stand in front of your closet and imagine stylish, creative Venus helping you to throw out what doesn't work.

Here are some other ways to address this wonderful maker of magic while keeping her indulgent side under wraps.

- "Venus, beautiful goddess of love, money, and creativity, it's now time for you to endow me with all your positive attributes. Of course it's wonderful to indulge oneself, but beautiful things are always better as a reward for accomplishment, no matter how small."

Balancing Your Orbit

- "No, Venus, you cannot justify why the world should wait on you."
- "No, you cannot dishonor this wonderful body that I inhabit by behaving in a manner that is unworthy of you."
- "Venus, I do want love in my life, and you will begin right now to help me attain it!"
- "You will help give me the consciousness to take care of myself and attend to my wonderful body as the beautiful temple it is."
- "You will heighten my ability to express creativity and my love of the arts."
- "You will bring love and material abundance into my life by weaving your spell to create real magic for me now!"

Be sure to take Venus shopping. Take her to the gym. She won't be pleased, because it will appear like too much hard work to her. Don't worry; let her take note of all those wonderful bodies and tell her that even goddesses have to work at it! She'll get the picture. You'll probably need Mars for the physical energy, so take him along too.

Make sure that she's paying attention when you're talking and/or listening to your stockbroker. Venus can smell a good investment a mile away. Also, be certain to take her to the bank when you need a loan; she attracts money and can smooth any situation when she thinks that there's money within her reach.

Summon all her power when you are working on a creative project. Take her to voice class, acting class, and public speaking events (you will need to drag Mercury along, too). Tell her to bring all of her magic into play.

Look deep into your eyes in the mirror and know that Venus has the power to attract love. She knows more than any other planet how to give and how to receive love. Tell her you are ready: "Venus, I am ready to receive love and abundance in my life. Use your magic, and I will respond by allowing all your creative and loving attributes to shine."

Kathy Kerston

MEET MARS
THE DANCING WARRIOR.

Known as Ares by the Greeks, Mars, the god of action, is aggressive, restless, and turbulent. He is also called the god of war. This son of Jupiter (mighty Zeus to the Greeks) is definitely not a favorite with his father, who cannot tolerate his emotional, irrational, and frenzied ways. Mars craves immediate action, be it war or passionate sex, and seldom, if ever, thinks things out before he acts. For all his bravado, he can be a bully and a braggart, but with all his daring, he seldom wins a battle. He rushes in with emotions and no common sense. However, like every other planet, there is another side.

There is a wonderful story about Mars that few are aware of. You see, Mars is not only a warrior, but a dancer as well. The altered states attained by runners and the whirling dervishes demonstrate the positive energy of Mars, as do the dancelike moves of martial artists, which are designed not so much for war, but to avoid it.

When the passion of anger is transmuted, as in dance, it rises up from the base chakra (*energy centers in the body that begin at the base of the spine up to the crown of the head*), and when it arrives at the heart chakra, an incredible thing happens. The energy is transmuted into love, which then stimulates the immune system, and a feeling of joy or euphoria sweeps through, similar to the runner's high.

When you are angry, dance, whirl if you can, and you will literally feel the energy change. It is in the physical that Mars expresses himself best, for without his energy, no daring deeds would be performed, no marathons run, no mountains climbed, no passions aroused. Without the energy of

Mars, life would be dull and there would be no lover for Venus. Mars needs to be coaxed into using all this energy for things such as sports, physical labor, and any endeavor needing courage, action, and physical energy, and then all is well.

Here's when to call on Mars:

- When you need to give Venus a push. Say to Mars, "Take it easy, don't rush, turn on your passion." Imagine this incredibly good-looking god blowing in your ear and encouraging you into a romance or a creative endeavor.
- When courage is the order of the day. See yourself standing with the warrior god. "Mars, give me your courage and your strength." See him hand you his sword, and feel the strength of your conviction flowing through you.
- When you need to take action and inertia can no longer be tolerated. Imagine yourself lying on the couch, and see Mars standing there. "Get up," he says. "I will empower you with lots of energy. We need to take action." See yourself smiling; feel the energy rush through you as he takes your hand and leaves you feeling invigorated and enthusiastic.
- When you want to engage in sports activity or start a training program at the gym. Imagine yourself performing the activity. See Mars as your coach, and feel his energy and enthusiasm flowing through you. "Let's go, Mars; it is action time."
- When you want to coach little league or go white-water rafting. See yourself in a boat or on the field. Let yourself feel the strength and courage of Mars. See him with you as you perform or direct with great athletic ability.
- When you want to start building that cabin you promised yourself or make those home improvements. Mars will be the one to supply you with all the energy you need. Just be certain to mention that you have plenty of time so he doesn't make you rush; he

can be accident-prone when impatient. See yourself considering the project. Imagine Mars, this strong athletic guy who can lift anything, waiting for your instructions. "Hi, Mars. Let's get ready. I know that you can perform all this work with boundless energy at a steady and safe pace." See him doing a job, and watch in your mind's eye as he carefully and efficiently performs the task.
- When you need to make changes in your life that will bring about a more positive environment. I refer to him as the cutting planet, for he cuts the things out of your life that are no longer needed. Imagine saying to Mars, "Give me the courage to let go from my life those people, thoughts, and attitudes that are no longer positive and healthy for me." Imagine him taking his sword and cutting through the air, and allow yourself to feel the freedom as you let go.

If you find yourself arguing too much, say to Mars, "Let's get something straight, this is not a war, oh mighty warrior; it's time for peace. Now, you can express all of your emotional, pent-up energy in those things in my life that are important to me." Tell Mars loud and clear what your expectations are of him:

- "You will give me courage and energy to accomplish the tasks that I have undertaken."
- "You will make me walk tall as a warrior, strengthening me to battle those things in myself that hold me back from being the best that I can be."
- "Stop bragging and help me take some action!"
- "You will direct my turbulent emotions to express themselves in the dance of life, but it will be my choice of exercise and creative endeavors."

- "You will enhance my passionate ability to love, not only people, but those things in life which add zest to it.
- "I will be certain to honor the change in your energy from warmonger to the god of positive action."

Some indications that Mars is out of control are bumping into things and generally seeming accident-prone, acting like a bully, running fevers, behaving impatiently, or flying off the handle at the drop of a hat. It's time to get hold of the situation by telling him very firmly that his energy is to be used to enhance life, and then, with a smile, invite him to dance.

If you are home alone, whirl around, dance, and feel the anger being transmuted into constructive and positive energy. When you are not at home, think of yourself dancing. Imagine your body enjoying the accelerating feeling of whirling, springing, and dancing.

You will be very surprised at what this can accomplish. When you invite Mars to dance, either your energy increases or your anger subsides, and a great feeling of joy is the reward. And by all means, don't forget the flattery! Tell him he's brave, energetic, and wonderful. Flattery wins. Tell him he's a great lover, although that's debatable because, without a little help, he's in too much of a hurry! Most of all have fun with him!

MEET JUPITER
THE GREAT BENEFACTOR

The Romans knew powerful and dramatic Zeus, Lord of Olympus, as Jupiter. The name is also used for the planet that depicts his attributes. After taking the throne from his father, Saturn, and rescuing his siblings, Jupiter decided that he and his two brothers, Pluto and Neptune, should draw lots to divvy up the world. Jupiter drew the sky and became known as the sky god. The earth was considered to be public domain, but since Jupiter had such a great view of it all from the sky, he decided he could do a terrific job ruling that as well. Neptune was given the oceans and seas, while Pluto was given the underworld.

As was his father, Saturn, and his grandfather, Uranus, he followed in the family tradition as a male chauvinist. When he was busy dividing up the universe, he totally ignored the rights of his sisters. Jupiter's lack of consideration for women went so far as to allow Pluto to kidnap his own daughter, Persephone, and take her to the underworld to become his wife. Jupiter then added insult to injury by lying to Persephone's mother, Demeter, as to her whereabouts.

For the most part, Jupiter has a gregarious and generous nature, and in his most fatherly moments, he gave the rulership of the Sun to his son, Apollo, and the Moon to Apollo's twin sister, Diana. He trusted Athena with his thunderbolt and carried his son, Dionysus, in his hip until he was old enough to be born. Although he was generous with his children, he made many promises that he didn't keep, as he was off somewhere enjoying himself.

As a husband, he took his gregarious and generous nature to an extreme that no wife could appreciate. He was a philanderer, and his many liaisons involved not only goddesses, but mortals.

Jupiter also has a temper. When he is angry, he roars like a lion in the halls of Olympus and bangs his fist on the table. However, his heart is big, his laugh infectious, and his generosity unbounded.

In astrology he rules the ninth sector, an area that covers such things as religion, philosophy, the higher self, law, higher education, travel and foreign places, politics, publishing, advertising, and the media.

Jupiter is the one who gives us faith and optimism, which opens the door to a more abundant life. While Venus rules love and money, Jupiter brings these things and more; he adds joy. He restores the ability to laugh after adversity and gives us the will to try again!

You know it is time to call on Jupiter when you are experiencing any of the following situations:

- When your soul needs to be lifted. I imagine Jupiter as a tall, handsome, and majestic figure wearing a deep purple robe. Though a deep sense of the spiritual surrounds him, he doesn't take himself too seriously. He knows that spiritual joy and laughter feed the soul. Imagine Jupiter taking off his cloak and placing it around you. Feel the peace and joy flow through you as you accept this gift. As he takes back his cloak, he tells you that the power of this garment is now within you; all you have to do is close your eyes and imagine it, and you will be filled with the awareness that you can access this joy whenever you wish. Faith is Jupiter's gift, and he has now endowed you with a knowing that surpasses the ordinary belief system.
- When you need to know that you are not alone. Imagine this happy-go-lucky god and ask him to keep you company. No one can lift your spirits like him.

- When your faith and optimism are in need of a boost. Jupiter castrates fear, laughs at adversity, and renews the spirit in the twinkling of an eye. See Jupiter in your mind's eye. See the situation where you need to feel confident and have faith in yourself. See Jupiter handing you a scepter, which he instructs you to hold high. Imagine it sending out rays of light that banish your doubts, and then laugh, loud and boisterous.
- When you need inner faith to accomplish your goals. Imagine the task you need to do to achieve your goals. See Jupiter place his cloak around you and his scepter in your hand. Feel the faith flow through you and know that you can accomplish these goals, for Jupiter, with all his gifts, is at your side.
- When you have a legal situation. See him at your side as the judge in his cloak, and know that he rules justly. Ask him to be with you if you need to go to court or if you have to sign legal papers.
- When you need to travel to foreign countries. Bring him along since he loves to travel. Tell Jupiter it is time for adventure. Ask him to orchestrate situations where language will not be a problem. Tell him you are ready for more knowledge about your world and that you are optimistic about the experiences you will have on this trip.
- When you want to learn a foreign language. Tell Jupiter that you know he can understand all languages and you would like his assistance at learning this one. See yourself sitting with him and conversing in that language, feeling amazed at how easily you are speaking and comprehending.
- When you want to have your work published. Ask Jupiter to guide you to the right source to publish your manuscript. See yourself sitting with Jupiter behind you, guiding you as to where to submit it. See yourself sending it out, and feel the joy when you know it is accepted.

Invite him to weddings and ceremonies, because he loves all the pomp and will add to the revelry. See Jupiter in all his attire; ask him to add his spiritual essence to the occasion, as well as his sense of fun and gaiety.

Whenever you study philosophy, mythology or walk the path of the mystic, sense him close. Jupiter's faith surpasses the written word, but it is the written word that sometimes speaks to the soul. When you are studying or choosing to explore a spiritual path, ask Jupiter to be your guide, so that you will know what is right for you at this time in your life.

Invite him along when you want to gamble, but remember he can exaggerate, so be sure to quit while you're ahead! See Jupiter ready to have fun, and see his confidence that he is going to win. Tell him, "We are going to have fun and win, and know when to quit." You had better have Saturn in the background in case he needs his father's wisdom.

So now that you know what Jupiter has to offer, it's time to tell him your expectations:

- "Jupiter, try not to laugh at everything; not all things are funny! I know you love to exaggerate, but from now on …"
- "You will give me faith and the belief in my ability to reach the stars."
- "You will now bring joy and abundance into all areas of my life."
- "You will remove all the foolish dramas from my life, and replace them with splendor."
- "You will lift me up to my higher self so that all the spiritual love inside of me shines like a beacon into the world."
- "You will assist me so that I can lighten the paths of my fellow men with a kind word, deed, or smile."
- "While you are doing these things, there will be lightness in my step and the light of laughter in my eyes; my spirit will soar, and I will climb any mountain I choose with confidence."
- "The thunderbolts that you let loose will be states of awareness."
- "I will enter the halls of learning and travel far."

- "I will understand those from different cultural or religious backgrounds."

Most of all, Jupiter is the planet to call on every day. He will help to build your sense of joy and faith, both of which banish fear. Just like the mighty Zeus, you too can laugh at mistakes and go forward to do great things.

Jupiter adds a royal touch to everything he does, and while always retaining his dignity, he laughs. His confidence and wonderful sense of humor allow him to forgive very easily. This is because he recognizes that mistakes are a part of life, and to forgive, even yourself, puts you on the road to freedom. Complaining about things that cannot be changed not only wastes time and energy, but also robs your life of joy and pleasure. So wave to Jupiter and laugh with him; he will always be there to lift you up!

MEET SATURN
THE TEACHER

Known to the Greeks as Cronus, Saturn was the ruler of Olympus until his son Jupiter dethroned him.

Saturn claimed his position as the ruler of Olympus through force by castrating and dethroning his father, Uranus. Because of this story, I call Saturn the paranoid planet. Why? Because what we obtain by force always leaves us with the fear of losing it, sometimes in the same manner we obtained it.

Serious, suspicious, and paranoid about the same thing happening to him, Saturn devoured most of his children so that they could not grow up and dethrone him. Jupiter was spared this fate because his mother, Rhea, encouraged by her mother-in-law, hid him and then tricked her husband by feeding him a stone wrapped in a blanket. Bon appetite, Saturn!

Saturn ruled with an iron fist and meted out justice with such exactness that there was no room for compassion or understanding, yet many sources refer to this as the golden age.

In Saturn's world, everything is black and white. The material world is the only thing he understands. Driven by a burning ambition to succeed, he really believes that without him directing it, the world cannot survive. He's bound and determined to get to the top and hold that position regardless of the price to others, and even at times, to himself. (Sound like anyone you know?) Saturn feels that he has the responsibility of the world on his shoulders. He may also have the tendency to think of himself as the sacrificial lamb in any given situation.

The other side of Saturn became evident when, after his son Jupiter dethroned him, he realized how foolish he had been. As the sense of pride for his son swept through him, his paranoia turned to wisdom. Because Saturn rules old age, it is thought that we acquire wisdom as we age, though sometimes it comes much earlier, in moments of great illumination and awareness.

We should remember, though, that wisdom came once Saturn saw the foolishness of resisting change. Those who resist the new order and want to hold on to the old ways are blocking the gift of wisdom.

This is not unlike the son who takes over his father's business. The father is convinced his son can't do a job as well as he did, or subconsciously doesn't want his son to do better than him. Yet when the father sees his son's accomplishments, he is filled with pride. Enter wisdom!

Saturn rules gravity and everything that needs a solid base and foundation. Saturn is a cold planet that rules iron ore and metals that are strong and unbending.

Where Saturn is situated in an individuals chart is where these attitudes of resistance tend to express themselves. OK, so you wonder why anyone in the world would ever want to call on this paranoid fellow! Well, believe it or not, we all need him sometime. Here are some very good times to talk to him:

- When you are feeling scattered, airy, and ungrounded. When practicality has flown out the window and you are in need of stability right now, it is time to have a talk with this fellow. I Imagine Saturn as a wise but stern old man with a long white beard. From a distance he looks rather menacing, but when you get up close, if you are brave enough, you see the twinkle in his eyes. Ask him for wisdom; tell him you want stability in any given situation. Say to him, "Saturn, I am feeling off kilter; ground me with your practicality, and give me the wisdom to handle all situations (especially this one) with maturity and efficiency."

Balancing Your Orbit

- When you're going to build any structure. Imagine Saturn with plans or drawings in hand and say to him, "Wonderful architect, be with me through this project; give me the wisdom of your knowledge in all phases of this building project. Keep me focused, and help me make wise decisions."
- When you want to start a corporation, a business or anything that you want to last. Ask Saturn to be your CEO. See him sitting at the board meetings or standing beside you as you make your business decisions. Ask Saturn to lay a solid foundation to this endeavor so that it will grow and endure for as long as you wish.

Outside of the business arena, ask him to be present when there's a need for level, practical, and unemotional decisions to be made. Ask Saturn to give you a cool and unencumbered mental attitude so that you can make decisions in an executive manner.

You need him when both wisdom and patience are required. Ask Saturn to give you the patience while you exercise his wisdom in this situation. See him sitting in a peaceful state and hear him say that all is in divine order; then know that your patience and wisdom will pay off.

Saturn has a particular affinity for the elderly, and demands that their rights be respected. Yes, you too will grow old. So take him along when you want respect or when you are seeking it for others.

Most of all, know that Saturn is an ally who generates great wisdom and possesses amazing longevity. Talk to Saturn and tell him your expectations of him:

- "Saturn, stop oppressing me! Just because you think of nothing but work and getting to the top, that doesn't mean everyone else has to. Listen, you old devil, and understand me clearly."
- "You will keep your paranoia to yourself, for I do not like being the sacrificial lamb. You hear me? I want no part of it."

- "You, my wise friend, will now give me structure, organization, persistence, and determination. All these will be clothed in wisdom."
- "You will lay a sure and solid foundation for me in all of my endeavors."
- "In all factions of my life, you will bring me permanence and stability now!"

Saturn respects those who accept responsibility, and he rewards those who persevere with wisdom. As time passes, he is aware when we have been diligent, and he blesses us with a sense of humor. Saturn knows that putting responsibility first brings great freedom and the opportunity to enjoy old age. Taking care of your retirement needs could be one way of describing the responsibility, as could taking care of your health. After the serious stuff, however, he wants to catch up on all the humor and fun he missed in his youth. We find him growing roses, fishing, and cooking up a gourmet meal. Therefore, he is our friend in our later years. So work with him in your youth, and you'll have a great ally for life.

MEET URANUS
THE GREAT AWAKENER

Uranus was the first ruler of Olympus. He was the sky god who married Gaea, the earth. He, like his son Saturn, did away with most of his children so that they would not dethrone him. Unlike Saturn, who, you'll remember, devoured his offspring, Uranus was not quite so vicious. Instead he chose to bury his children in the earth. After reading about Saturn, you, along with Uranus, might wonder why Gaea rescued Saturn and encouraged him to castrate his father, an act for which she offered Saturn the throne, even if it wasn't hers to offer.

Once Saturn dethroned Uranus, Uranus felt a tremendous sense of freedom. Saturn claimed the throne with such speed that Uranus felt as though a bolt of lightning hit him, bringing him freedom and enlightenment. In his exuberance, he lit up the sky and caused sudden and unexpected events to occur so that mankind could also experience this same sense of awakening and freedom. This is why Uranus in astrology is called the Great Awakener, hence the statement, "Do you have to be hit with a bolt of lightening?"

Uranus felt that sense of freedom because he had buried his creative genius in the earth, afraid it would take over the comfortable position he held, but Gaea knew it needed to be released, and the castration brought forth from the sea the most powerful of all the goddesses, Aphrodite (Venus).

Uranus transcends the mundane mind, Mercury's domain, and brings flashes of genius, clairvoyance, and enlightenment. Therefore, Uranus rules the higher state of consciousness.

In astrology, Uranus is considered the higher octave of Mercury and rules the eleventh house, the area of hopes, dreams, and wishes. Since Mercury rules the mundane mind, it becomes apparent that going up an octave will give us higher communication, clairvoyance, or access to anything that is futuristic.

Uranus the inventor is always ahead of the times. In order to achieve our dreams and wishes, we have to unearth the buried treasures that lie deep within. We have to be castrated from the fears that these wishes will take us to new heights and unchartered waters that could make us insecure.

Uranus's effect on us is like being pushed out of a room that we have lived in for a long time, a room with heavy blinds on the windows and a limited amount of light. As we are pushed out into the bright sunlight, we are traumatized, as the light burns our eyes, yet as we adjust to the change, we see a glorious world we didn't know existed and feel the thrill of discovery.

All of us are being affected more and more by this planet, for we have entered the age of Aquarius, the sign ruled by this planet, and its urge for change and freedom cannot be ignored. All the technological advances are a result of entering this age. On a personal level, the energy of this planet is moving us all into a state of enlightenment and awakening. This awakening brings freedom. Information, tools, and teachers are emerging everywhere, bringing the message of freedom from the beliefs that has held us for so long in bondage. Movies like *What the Bleep* and *The Secret*, to name two. Messages from Abraham, channeled through Ester Hicks, concerning the law of attraction and emotional freedom technique (EFT), a system that uses acupuncture points to release old traumas. Check out www.emofree.com. These are some of the Aquarian tools now available.

In the Piscean age, we learned about love, compassion, and self-sacrifice. It was the time of the martyr, a time when the soul learned to express itself in beauty and art. However, as in everything where we overcompensate, the teaching of self-sacrifice brought the birth of codependency and various religions that entrenched us in guilt. Now, in the age of Aquarius, the message is, "I am going to help you help yourself." Before we can help others, first we have to help ourselves get into the right space, and sometimes we do both at the same time.

The old saying is, "We teach that which we need to learn most." It is always prudent to go with the flow with Uranus. Because of the desire for change, we have to be careful that we don't seek change just for the sake of change, yet also remain open to it as it presents itself.

Whenever Uranus deems we should be enlightened, he has a habit of propelling us into new and uncharted territory, often quite quickly and without warning. An example would be when you have a job in the morning and, quite unexpectedly, you don't have one in the evening. This only happens if you are stuck or unhappy.

There is a saying that most of us astrologers use when referring to Uranus. "He is going to force you to change, one way or the other—either 'nice and easy' or 'kicking and screaming.'" Either way, Uranus makes sure that we are freed from limiting conditions. If you like an exciting ride through life, then Uranus is your planet. I call him the thrill planet. If you feel him getting too rough, say, "Sure, Uranus, I want enlightenment and freedom, but you don't have to pull the rug out from beneath me to achieve this state. Why is it necessary for me to give up everything of substance in my life to learn the lesson of detachment?"

When should you call on Uranus? Speak to him when you find yourself stuck in a rut. I imagine Uranus as a young man dressed in an iridescent tunic with a crystal wand that can charge a battery or light up the sky. Say to Uranus, "I want out of this rut; heighten my intuition so that, like you, I can free myself from this self-imposed situation. But hold on, don't catapult me there; use that wand like the good witch, and cast your spell of exciting discovery."

When you can't see the forest for the trees, talk to Uranus. Imagine yourself in the situation and ask that Uranus bring you a brilliant awareness of what to do. Here are some examples of when Uranus might be of help.

- When you feel that life has you bound up in a situation where you cannot see a way out. Tell Uranus, "It's time to free myself from this situation; bring me the tools and awareness necessary to make these changes. Do this in an enlightened way through my intuition."
- When you know that your thinking is stuck, but you can't seem to change. Speak to Uranus; say to him, " I am ready for change; I am open to new and innovative ideas that will bring freedom and variety into my life."
- When you are going through a divorce. "I am ready to release my partner in light and love so that we both can be free to explore new experiences; bring this situation in my life to a quick and positive conclusion."
- When you need to let go of your children because they are either moving out, going to college or getting married. Tell Uranus you are freeing your offspring to explore new and exciting events in their lives. Say to him, "Now that I am releasing my child (or children), I know that you will bring new and stimulating experiences into my life, and I am ready."

When you know that you can't stay in that job or that relationship any longer, tell him that you are ready to start detaching right now. Tell him also that you would like to detach yourself from his lunacy, his erratic nature, and his temper tantrums! That should get his attention! Be insistent when you tell Uranus what you want:

- "You will light up my vision so that I can see the trends of the future clearly now."
- "You will now quicken my mind so that it will conceive concepts that will bring me deep inner personal freedom."
- "I will invent new and unique ideas for improving my life and the lives of others."

- "From now on, all your surprises will be good, and I will arrive at a state of awareness without being scared half out of my wits."
- "I will now enter into a state of peace and brotherhood. I will see differences as wonderful aspects of humanity, not as things that separate."
- "I will now leave behind all that has bound my spirit and move on to great adventures."

It's time now for you to welcome freedom into your life, but call the shots on how it will occur! Let your higher mind and the wonderful inventor Uranus show you the way! Just let him know you're ready; give him directions, take a deep breath, and leap. Skydiving has nothing on this!

MEET NEPTUNE
THE MASTER OF ILLUSION

Neptune was known to the Greeks as Poseidon, ruler of the vast oceans. When he and his brothers drew lots to divide up the universe, Neptune drew the watery domain as his kingdom. Neptune's nature is nebulous, like that of the sea—one minute calm, and the next, violent and destructive. His mysterious nature is often associated with magic and alchemy.

Neptune can, at times, have a hypnotic effect, which can create illusions or illumination. Just as he can increase or decrease the boundaries of the oceans at his will, creating the impression that something is what it is not, Neptune can create this same effect in your life.

Whenever Neptune was calm and in a benevolent mood, he would create miracles, very much in evidence in the age of Pisces, the sign he has rulership over, which would upset Saturn because this defied Saturn's sense of reality. Saturn had no liking for Neptune, for he didn't understand miracles; he viewed Neptune as irrational, especially when his power of illusion caused men to become intoxicated.

Neptune, like Mars and Jupiter, had a temper. He was also a philanderer like his brother Jupiter (Zeus).

There was another side of Neptune that was seldom observed, that of the god who could calm the troubled sea and visit the temples where his worshipers prayed, where he would grant their wishes. He could cause an earthquake to turn a lake into dry land or create a lake in the desert. Neptune also appointed the fixed stars Castor and Pollux to calm the stormy seas and protect the sailors.

Balancing Your Orbit

It was Neptune's domain that gave birth, along with the sperm of Uranus, to the goddess Aphrodite (Venus). The combination of the Neptune/Venus energy can cause incredible miracles, wondrous works of art, and love and compassion that surpasses all understanding. He touches Venus's creations with magic and makes her powers of love go far beyond the boundaries of the physical, into a communion with the soul, hence, Venus is exalted in Pisces, the sign ruled by Neptune.

Neptune is limitless. Just as you can freeze water and then walk on it, or boil it so that it becomes vapor and flies away, Neptune can drown you in a spiritual and euphoric fog or make you get strung out on drugs and alcohol in seeking that euphoric place that can only be accessed from the awakening of Uranus and the loving or creative power of Venus.

I imagine Neptune as an older deity looking a little rough on the edges, with long hair and an unruly beard, but gentle and compassionate eyes. You may wonder, if Neptune is so nebulous and so moody, how do I know he's listening? Not to worry, he hears you, especially when you're speaking from your heart.

- When you want to be creative and have already called in Venus. Ask Neptune to assist by adding even more imagination to the creative endeavor. Visualize yourself about to begin whatever creative project you are considering; then imagine Neptune whispering in Venus's ear, and watch her create like never before. Hear Neptune calling you to join them; feel the creative energy flowing through you, and see yourself accomplishing your goal.
- When you are meditating or enhancing your spiritual or psychic awareness. Imagine that you are sitting by water, and ask Neptune to join you; as you gaze into the water, let your mundane mind be calm. Ask Neptune to enhance your state of meditation and your psychic ability. Look deeply into his compassionate eyes, and feel the spiritual love that is flowing to you. Know that the peace will remain with you.

- When you need a miracle. Visualize the situation that you want to be miraculously transformed, and then call on Neptune. Say, " I ask with love and compassion that this situation be touched by the healing power of love, the energy that can transform anything." Sit quietly with the scene in your mind's eye, and know that Neptune is awakening the power within you to perform miracles.
- When your emotions are working overtime. While sitting in meditation, invite Neptune to calm the sea of emotion that is churning inside you. If meditation is not feasible, pick a trigger point on your body, usually a finger thumb position, any that feels right for you, and mentally imagine that you are looking at a stormy sea. While breathing deeply, see it becoming calm.
- When you need to enhance your compassion. Close your eyes and see the image of Neptune. See beyond his rough exterior and look deep into those loving and compassionate eyes. "Yes, Neptune, I am awakening the compassion that I know resides in me." Sit with this until you feel it.

Bring him close in any situation where healing is desired. Know that he is there with you, reminding you of your own gift of healing. Make certain to ask him along on a cruise, and ask him to protect you when swimming or performing any water sport. Take him, along with Saturn and Mercury, to the AA meeting, to help shatter the illusions that alcohol created. Most of all, ask him to banish all negative illusions from your life.

When you feel as if you're afloat and your life is turbulent, call on Neptune by saying, "Calm down, you crazy loon. You have such an incredible ability to create spiritual peace, no one can perform miracles like you. No one can turn the tides of fate like you, so let's get going. Stop making my head spin with fanciful tales that have no substance. Leave the martini alone, and throw away the marijuana. Stop distorting the facts. You know more than anyone that negative illusions can ruin lives. I will get high on love."

Now that you are more familiar with Neptune's nature, tell him how you'd like his presence to manifest itself in your life:

- "You will give me illumination and increase my psychic awareness."
- "You will awaken in me the knowledge that I, too, can heal and create miracles."
- "You will give me a photographic mind when I choose."
- "You will sharpen my extrasensory receptors so that I can see the beauty in all things."
- "You will enhance my creative powers."
- "You will heighten my feelings of compassion in the right situations."
- "You will begin the halcyon days of my life right now."

Tell Neptune loud and clear to illuminate your mind and to perform miracles in your life. Don't be shy, demand it. Remember it is all about energy and intension. To the casual observer, it will seem that you simply have incredible luck!

MEET PLUTO
THE GREAT TRANSFORMER

In Greek mythology, Pluto was known as Hades. When Jupiter rescued his brothers, and the universe was divided up, Pluto got the underworld, a place of great riches. Gold, diamonds, and all manner of precious materials are all buried in the earth, but to reach those riches, metaphorically speaking, you have to make the journey into Pluto's domain.

Most people are profoundly afraid of this journey, for they know that Pluto is a serious god, with an intense, penetrating personality, who resides in the domain of the dead, where souls rest between incarnations.

It was believed that those who ventured into the underworld never returned. In a sense, that's true, for they never returned the same as they had been before they left. The underworld is used as a metaphor for our deep subconscious, where we all must journey for any real change to take place. That's why Pluto is referred to as the great transformer.

Pluto demands a transformation, and he will push until this transformation occurs. His method is not unlike the transformation from the caterpillar to the butterfly. Pluto, in his way, forces us to build a cocoon, like the caterpillar, which, upon entering, must die from its old way to become a butterfly.

Deep transformation is always achieved in Pluto's domain. He pushes us down, sometimes into the depths of despair and sorrow, for he, recognizes the ruts we can fall into, and knows that sometimes this is the only way we will transform. It is through this painful experience that we will become aware of our own power.

Balancing Your Orbit

Our pain and suffering are not in vain, as they will ultimately bring renewal and riches. When we finally emerge from the darkness into the sunlight, we are as the phoenix, rising out of the ashes of our death to live anew. Pluto offers the cornucopia, overflowing with the fruits and riches of life, as the reward for going deep within ourselves and returning much richer for the experience.

Once this transformation has taken place, we are able to soar through the sky, viewing the world from a higher vantage point. Wow, what a world!

Remember that Mercury is the only one who has free access to come and go in Pluto's domain. Mercury rules how we think and what we believe, so you will want his company when you begin this journey, for he knows the way in as well as the way out.

Now that you have traveled down into Pluto's underworld and survived, it's time for fun. It doesn't have to be painful to learn that life was not meant to be a struggle. You're probably wondering, and sensibly I may add, why you would want to go and commune with this dark, mysterious guy.

In astrology Pluto rules the eighth house, the sector that rules death and regeneration. It also rules other people's values. I call Pluto the control freak because he doesn't let you out of his domain; the truth is he gives you back your power, and when you have that power, you soar out of there on swift wings. Pluto demands, he doesn't ask, for a death and regeneration of attitude. He teaches us about self-control. When we have control of ourselves, we do not need to control others. The need to control others always stems from the fear of losing control of one's self. It's for your own good! Don't be intimidated by his control tactics. Don't you want your power back?

Go into the underworld with Pluto when you need to tap into that deep inner power, and remember that you are calling the shots now. If you are experiencing the dark night of the soul, you are in Pluto's domain. The power to change our lives is truly in our hands. You wrote this script, your astrology chart, and you have the power to change it.

I imagine Pluto as a tall, handsome, serious-looking fellow, a dark knight all dressed in black. He wears a black helmet and a mask, and you can only see his eyes. I know that under that black clothing lies a being of light so bright that we couldn't stand to view it with our mortal eyes, therefore we may only see his brilliance as reflected in others. Only after we have made our transition into the spirit world or look into Pluto's eyes will we be truly able to see that light. For now, know that it is there guiding you.

Here's when you need Pluto's assistance:

- When you know that it is time to let go of control over anything outside of yourself. Visualize this magnificent knight and ask him to shine some of his light into your awareness so that you can release the need to control. See yourself in a situation where you want this to happen, and see yourself calm and confident, knowing that everything is in order. Feel the satisfaction flow through you as you release the need to control.
- When you want profound psychological changes. Imagine Pluto inviting you into his domain. You may feel a little scared, for you have to go down these dark steps with very little light, but you have invited Mercury to journey with you, for you are ready to change your thinking and old beliefs and perceptions. You enter a dark, cold room, lit only by torchlight. You sit on a thronelike seat, while Pluto sits on one opposite. Pluto asks if you are ready to let die those old beliefs that have outworn their need, and you say, "Pluto, I am here because I want to transform my life. I release my need to control. I know that when I have self-control, I have no need to control anyone else and nobody can control me. My mind is now ready to soar to new heights." Pluto asks you to come closer to him. As you approach, he narrows his eyes so that you get just a glimpse. He tells you that the light you see is the light of your soul, and a

feeling of euphoria sweeps through you. You know you will never be the same.
- When you've had enough of crawling around like a caterpillar and are ready to become a butterfly. Call upon Pluto and tell him you are ready to make the journey of transformation. "I have had enough, Pluto. It has to be better than this (and believe me it is). I am ready, so take my hand, and let's go."

When someone you know has left this world and you need understanding, imagine yourself taking the journey into the underworld, only this time as you pass through the dark chamber, a door opens into an incredibly beautiful place. Imagine your loved one there and ask Pluto for the understanding that this is only a place of transition. Have a conversation with your loved one and maybe tell them things that you never got a chance to say. Bless them and release them. Pluto will call Mercury to escort you back.

When you feel the need to rise from the depths of despair, speak to Pluto and say, "Lord of the underworld, I have stayed here too long, I am now aware that it is time to emerge into the light. Make me aware of your transformative power so that I can begin a new and glorious life with the knowledge I have gained." Say to Pluto, "I have now learned your secret, my friend, and I am ready to journey with you."

Now that you've made his acquaintance, speak your intentions to him:

- "Trust me, I am no longer afraid. I have been down there with you before, but at those other times, I did not understand. It is now time for you to return my divine inheritance, and it will all flow to me in divine order!"
- "You will now give me back my power."
- "You will transform my life by making it richer in every way."

- "You will now bring wealth into my life in a variety of ways by making me aware of my own power."
- "You will give me the ability to help others transform their lives, not through control, but through example."
- "You will now renew every cell in my body, bringing me into a state of total health."
- "You will now erase any and all fear of death and bring with this change the knowledge that death is only a part of the process of renewal."

Remember the first stage of transformation is the caterpillar that becomes the butterfly. Wave to Pluto as you flutter your butterfly wings. Buy some flowers for your home and inhale the energy. Know that the next steps are: first, like the phoenix that rises out of the ashes; then, as the eagle, which flies higher than any other bird. Yes, that's you!

When it's truly time for transformation in any area of your life, and you'll decide when that is, call on Pluto's power and get your wings.

Additional Thoughts

Remember, we are created in our maker's image!

Jesus, our brother, teacher, and avatar, the one I am the most familiar with, said, "Unless you become as a little child, you cannot enter the kingdom of heaven" (Mark 18–3). Did you ever wonder what he meant? I believe he may have been referring to the fact that through playing and employing the imagination we allow ourselves to feel and see things without all of the complications we have picked up throughout our lives. We hold the keys to the door of our life, which, incidentally, is right in front of us!

I have heard many times that "the kingdom of heaven is within." That means heaven isn't somewhere else; it's right here, right now, and it's what we make of it! Welcome to the age of enlightenment and freedom.

The ancients believed that the Sun was the giver of life, and in fact, the Sun is the core of your experience in this incarnation. Most astrology books describe the positive and negative traits of each sign, but for the purposes of this book, we will focus only on a few of the gifts of your sun sign.

Direct the positive energy of the Sun by focusing on the gifts and talents of your sign and the planet that rules it. Claim that energy now.

ARIES: Ruled by **Mars**. This sign is given the gift of spontaneity. Bright. Brave. Adventurous. Curious. Lively. Childlike. Happy. Carefree. You are the naive child discovering the universe. You are the one at the front of the line. As you initiate and lead, don't look back to see who follows. That is not your job. Shine your light for all to see, and then move courageously forward.

TAURUS: Ruled by **Venus**. This lovely planet brings the solid side of her nature to the forefront in this earth sign. Motivated by love, she brings gifts of love and harmony. Steady. Persevering. Loving. Creative. Comforting. Patient. Nurturing. Intuitive. Build whatever you desire—business, a home, a relationship—with beauty and permanence in mind, and love will keep you warm.

GEMINI: Ruled by **Mercury**. The gifts of this planet are of the mind, the ability to communicate ideas. Change. Movement. Curiosity. Communication. Travel. Writing. Flexibility. Don't be deterred by those who remain stuck; love, laugh, talk, and keep moving. There are so many exciting things to learn and communicate. Strengthen your wings and fly.

CANCER: Ruled by the **Moon**. Emotional freedom is the gift that the Moon offers. Sensitive. Intuitive. Nurturing. Creative. Hospitable. Loyal. Caring. The gift here is to remember that caring doesn't mean carrying. Love and nurture your dreams. Love and nurture yourself, and the world will open wide its doors of unconditional love.

LEO: Ruled by the **Sun**. The energy to create is the gift of the Sun. Drama. Passion. Courage. Energy. Love. Strength. Endurance. You are not here to stay in the background. You are here to add love and color to the world. Be true to yourself, and enjoy your own creations. Be proud of your accomplishments and creations, but don't let them rule you, and you will be happy and successful in all you do.

VIRGO: Ruled by **Mercury.** Here, in an earth sign, Mercury focuses its gifts on research. Practical. Perceptive. Organized. Structured. Efficient. When the practical issues of life are organized and in their respective places, the freedom to explore new and innovative ideas are Mercury's gift. Take time to explore the world of ideas and travel. Take time in nature. Mercury is timeless, and in Virgo, you can stay forever young. Remember, when everything is in place, it's time to play.

LIBRA: Ruled by **Venus.** In this air sign, Venus is unlimited in its ability to create. Harmony. Relationships. Creativity. Art. Love. Don't hide your talent. Step forward and create in whatever medium you choose. It is important that you create a harmonious environment. Love what you do, and happiness will open its doors wide for you.

SCORPIO: Ruled by **Pluto** and **Mars.** Pluto's gifts are powerful and transformative, while Mars brings courage and action. Controlled. Determined. Penetrating. Observant. Intriguing. Sexy. Your ability to see what is below the surface makes you an excellent investigator. Turn on that passionate appeal. Look for the clues that lead to your own happiness; they are closer than you think.

SAGITTARIUS: Ruled by **Jupiter.** Faith. Optimism. Intuition. Joy. Abundance. Knowledge. Travel. These are Jupiter's gifts. Make the world your playground. Know that the gods love laughter. Listen to your inner guidance; honor your desire for knowledge and truth; speak your mind with kindness. Travel far in mind or body, and joy will always find you.

CAPRICORN: Ruled by **Saturn.** The gift of perseverance is bestowed on the natives of this sign. Steadfast. Cautious. Dependable. Solid. Capricorn is trying to get to the top of the mountain; an inner drive moves you. For what or where? You don't always know. Wisdom is Saturn's gift. Relax. Trust in and listen to your inner wisdom, and the universe will take you wherever you wish to go. Admire the view while you climb the mountain. Enjoy the ride. You're guaranteed to get there.

AQUARIUS: Ruled by **Uranus**. Independent. Unique. Intuitive. Inventive. Humanitarian. Nonconforming. These are a few of the words that describe this sign. Freedom is an inside job. How you think and what you believe determines if you are really free. Listen to your higher self. Take that higher road, and know that your dreams are as accessible as the air you breathe. Follow your inner guidance, not the pack, and the winds of fate will lift you high and carry you to the throne of your desires.

PISCES: Ruled by **Neptune**. Faith is the power that drives natives of this sign. Imaginative. Creative. Loving. Sensitive. Humanitarian. Spiritual. Believe in the impossible dream. Use your sensitivity to create wonderful works. Be a spiritual light, a beacon that throws its light out, not one that draws the moths. Love yourself, honor your gifts, and trust your intuition and Neptune will make all your dreams a realty.

Now that you have a clear idea of what the planets' energies are, and the gifts of your sun sign, you might want to send out a message to the universe in general. I usually do a mediation on the new moon in which I address the congress of the planets. Here is my script:

To the Congress of the Planets

As I center myself in love, I give thanks for all the support I have received. My body is healthier every day. My mind is clear, with positive and constructive thoughts. My emotions choose to be happy, contented, and grateful for all the blessings in my life. My emotions know the difference between love, compassion, and dependency. I am, however, coming before the heavenly planetary alignment today to clearly state, as a child of God, the behavior I demand from the planetary energies.

From the **Sun** I ask to receive life energy, chi, with vibrant health and a sunny disposition. I ask for vitality and perfect health that will shine forth in my appearance. I ask for the ability to radiate love and healing.

The **Moon** will heighten my intuition and let go of all memories that no longer serve my purpose. Give me an excellent memory for those things that I deem important. I demand that my nurturing nature be positive and that love be the force that rules my emotions.

Mercury, give me clear thinking and communication skills. Increase my ability to articulate and write, in a manner that is both simple and profound. Let me only sign papers and documents that are beneficial to me. Let me read every word and understand what I read. Let me understand foreign languages.

Venus, bring love, art, beauty, creativity, and abundance into my life. Give me magic so that through my talents, I will touch many lives and be used as an instrument for healing. Give me a marriage full of love, friendship, physical attraction, laughter, and joy, one where every moment we spend together is filled with caring and happiness, one where there is respect for each other's need for time apart. Give me a marriage where there is plenty of money for us both to fulfill our pleasures, as well as our services to mankind. Give me magic and miracles.

Mars, I demand courage, energy, and determination. You will give me this energy through your physical powers as a dancer, for the energy to dance is far longer-lasting than the energy of war.

Jupiter, I demand that you protect me and my family, as well as all those I love, from all physical harm. Always endow me with faith and optimism so that I may reach farther than I have ever reached into the heavenly spheres. Endow me with incredible luck and abundance so that I might not only enjoy this sojourn here and now, but be better able to serve others. Take me to see wonderful places on this earth, to witness miracles and to create them. Let me speak foreign languages and understand them. Let me always operate from my higher mind.

Saturn, oh wonderful teacher, now that Jupiter has taken your throne, you have the time to cultivate wisdom. Give me that wisdom now! Let me always be in the right place at the right time for the very best to happen in my life. Make all the timing in my life perfect. Give me a solid foundation and an anchor. Give me the structure and organization that will make my time freer.

Uranus, give me your freedom, the freedom from fear, limitations, and the ghosts of the past, freedom from religious and cultural ideas that are no longer applicable to my growth. Free me from the demands of the negative side of my ego and from the need to see the results of my efforts. Free me that I might be in the present while seeing the future. Give me your clairvoyance, your genius ideas, and your inventive talents. Give me the mastery of your inventions, the computer, telepathy, and air travel.

Neptune, maker of miracles, I thank God for the gifts you endowed me with: my imagination, my creative talents, and my capacity to love and forgive. I am now here to demand that you banish all illusions, that you give me the ability to create miracles. To heal body, mind and soul. Neptune, fate maker, I am rewriting my past so that I may create a new future, living backwards as does the magician. As I see the future, so will I change it. Take me on your astral travels with all consciousness so that I may bring information back with me. Neptune, filmmaker and artist, let me create with you an incredible work of magic.

Pluto, oh guardian of the gates of death, take off your dark disguise that I might look upon your angelic face of light. Without death there is no birth. Plant in me the seeds of regeneration so that as I lay my hands to heal, reach deep into the soul and transform the fear that resides there. Banish in me the fear of death. Give me back my powers of mastery, the first of which is the power over myself. I am now choosing, this very day, to take back the power that you are offering me. As you cast your light upon my life, to Mercury, Venus, Mars, Jupiter, and Saturn, I demand all the positive attributes from these planets. I demand that their negative side be transformed, through your energy, into positive and creative energy that benefits all who pass through my life.

I come before the committee today, and as I stand before you with full knowledge of what I am asking, I stand in the light of truth, love, and wisdom. I bear the light of truth in my heart and soul, ever ready to shine. Give me these gifts now, for they are my heritage, and I will use them well.

Now that you have a good idea of how these planetary energies work, you are ready to create new and wonderful situations in your life. These practices could be viewed as a sort of alchemy that transmutes the abstract ideas of planetary energies into concrete happenings. Setting the right time to perform these rituals and using the right materials—talisman, candles, incense, and such—strengthen the planets' presence in our lives to make positive changes.

Choose the day ruled by the planet you most want to invoke, and then choose the hour for another planet whose energy you might want to add. The day gives the main vibration, and the planet that rules the hour compliments it.

Day Rulerships
- **Sunday** The Sun
- **Monday** The Moon
- **Tuesday** Mars
- **Wednesday** Mercury
- **Thursday** Jupiter
- **Friday** Venus
- **Saturday** Saturn

The planet ruling the day always has rulership over the first hour beginning at sunrise. I use the Chaldean order for the planets' rulership of hours, which always follow in this order. **Sun, Venus, Mercury, Moon, Saturn, Jupiter, Mars.**

Let us say that you want to begin to write a passionate romantic novel. You could begin to write on a Wednesday, Mercury's day, for Mercury rules writing. You can then add the hour of Venus, which would be, depending on the time of the sunrise, most likely 2:00 p.m. or 9:00 p.m., if sunrise on that day was at 7:00 a.m. You could also begin your writing on a Friday, Venus's day, in the hour of Mercury. In this case, the hour following sunrise would be the Mercury hour, as Mercury follows the Venus hour. Or you could wait for Mars, the planet of passion, at noon.

Examples:

Wednesday: ruled by **Mercury.** Let's say that it is July and the run rises early: 6–7 a.m. would belong to Mercury; 7–8 a.m., the Moon; 8–9 a.m., Saturn; 9–10 a.m., Jupiter; 10–11 a.m., Mars; 11 a.m.–12 p.m., the Sun; 12–1 p.m., Venus; 1–2 p.m., Mercury. Everything then repeats.

Friday: ruled by **Venus.** 6–7 a.m., Venus; 7–8 a.m., Mercury; 8–9 a.m., the Moon; and so on.

If possible, wear the color of the planet you are invoking or wear the gemstone associated with the planet. You can create a talisman on the day of your ruling planet, and use it whenever you need energy, guidance, or clarity.

- **Sun** rules **Leo** and the color is **yellow.**
- **Moon** rules **Cancer** and the color is **white.**
- **Mercury** rules **Gemini** and **Virgo** and the color is **silver** (the colors for the moon and mercury are interchangeable).
- **Venus** rules **Taurus** and **Libra** and the color is **green.**
- **Mars** rules **Aries** and the color is **red.**
- **Saturn** rules **Capricorn** and the colors are **black** and **brown.**
- **Uranus** rules **Aquarius** and the colors are **iridescent hues.**
- **Neptune** rules **Pisces** and the colors are **aquamarine** and others associated with **water.**
- **Pluto** rules **Scorpio** and the colors are **crimson** and all **dark reds.**

Planet Metals and Gems
- **Sun** Gold, Diamond, Quartz Crystal

- **Moon** Silver, Moonstone, Pearl
- **Mercury** Platinum, Agate, Pumice
- **Venus** Copper, Jade, Coral, Lapis, Malachite
- **Mars** Steel, Ruby, Garnet, Bloodstone, Onyx
- **Jupiter** Tin, Topaz, Amethyst
- **Saturn** Iron, Lead, Garnet, Hematite
- **Uranus** Amazonite, Any iridescent stone
- **Neptune** No metal, Aquamarine, Amethyst, Mother of pearl
- **Pluto** Volcanic rocks, Ruby, Garnet

Balancing Your Orbit

Now that you have all the information, claim your power and allow joy to be the passionate force that drives your life. I have described these planets in their mythological roles. Use your imagination and have fun. Visualize yourself in the situation you wish to be, and then see and feel the desired result taking place. Claim back the power to create magic in your life. You deserve it.

Printed in the United States
205470BV00002B/532-654/P